JOANNA SVE...

THE SEVEN COLORS
OF MY LIFE

(Edited by Rose Terranova Cirigliano)
Published by

QUEENS   BROOKLYN   LONDON
ROME   SAN FRANCISCO

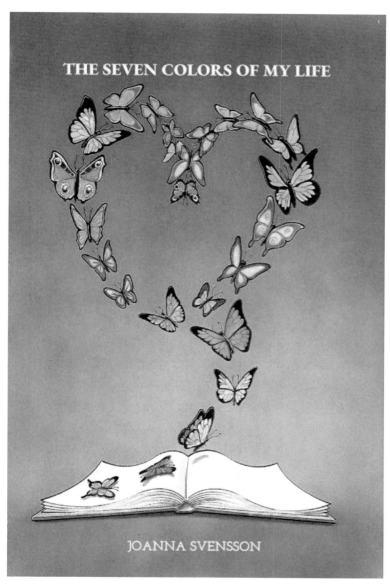

THE SEVEN COLORS OF MY LIFE

JOANNA SVENSSON

(cover by Per Josefsson)

Editor's Note
By Rose Terranova Cirigliano

*"To everything there is a season,
and a time for every purpose under heaven."*
(Eccl. 3:1)

It is a special season for Joanna Svensson. Writing for many years, but filled with self doubt, Joanna hesitated. And then she met the love of her life, and with that new found love her soul has burst forth in a celebration of words. Joanna's poems breathe on their own. The lines flow and the images caress your senses in a most exciting way.

You get caught up in the swell of her heart, and the dancing of her soul as it covers the page with some of the most beautiful words of love, and passion, and delight. This collection is filled with warmth and embraces the reader.

Snuggle on a couch by a fire, or watch the sunset with a glass of wine, and read Joanna's poems out loud. You will have to smile.

TABLE OF CONTENTS

Dedication

To my dearly beloved mother
Janina
who, unselfishly, with awesome power
fought your way through life.
Alone with four children
you managed to row
the boat ashore.
And despite all defeats
in life, you always saw lucky stars
scattered across the sky for each
and everyone of us!

Forever thank you!

Introduction

It is late in the evening. I turn on my reading lamp by my drawing board and sit myself down with a cup of coffee. In front of me I have a huge pile of Joanna's poetry.

In the starry sky millions of starbeams falls through my window and it seems like each star symbolizes a poem.

Out of all these I now have the painstakingly issue to pick out around seventy poems. This is a very tough task, because I have very warm feelings for all of them.

I can strongly feel Joanna's presence. She would have said: -The night time is very magical!

Joanna's lyrics are written straight from her heart. Where ever in the world you find her, it's always the voice of her heart and the words of her soul that she puts in full bloom in her poetry.

It is her delicate senses that owns the ability to unstrained capture and give life to all the wonderful things in life's manifold reality. As in:

> *"I have seen an angel being born*
> *Way up in the clear blue sky*
> *On a downy cloud*
> *Slowly it took form*
> *Its shape grew sharper*
> *Pulsating of life and light*

I felt it was born for me
To follow me
On my new path of life"

Or:

Freedom!
With fragrance from all the beautiful
flowers of spring
Is born today – at seven o'clock this
morning
Here in our garden
A wonderful, incredible feeling – has
filled my heart
When I saw the happy smile of the sun
And when the lovely greenery – the tiny
little brook
Had already whispered – babbled
About the arrival of freedom in my life!

where she, all the way from playful cheerfulness to subtle carefulness, balances between the whole wide world and her own little corner of it.

For each poem I find reflections of my soul mate, my spiritual cleavage. It feels like I am travelling along with her on her journey of life – decorated with happiness, sorrows, earnestness and sometimes fear.

Sometimes I wonder why she hasn't published more poems earlier. But maybe it is like Schopenhauer said when he divided writers into two categories:

"Those who writes for the cause and those who writes just for writing. The former have had thoughts and made experiences they want to tell us about, while the latter need money and therefor writes for money. They seldom contemplate"

In Joanna's case it is perfectly clear that she prefers quality before quantity. You can easily see how important it is for her to "paint with words", live out her feelings and, as often as possible, visit her endless archive of dreams and experiences.

Ever since early childhood Joanna has been writing down her feelings in short stories and poems. Her teacher in school often wanted to give Joanna two different grades for her essays; the highest possible for its contents - and another for her writing.

Even if this is a book filled with love poems and season poems, there have been periods in Joanna's life when dark clouds were covering her sun. Periods when she wrote many dark, heavy, gloomy and sometimes even rebellion and provocative poems.

But even in the most dreary ones, she has urged for hope, by, in the end of the poem "peak around the corner", "see the light in the tunnel" or "turn a new page".

In her poem "Tree of Life" she begins with:

> *"Your tree of life – is about to lose – its last leaves..."*
> *"All along you knew that this day would come..."*
> *"And then – the two last leaves falls from your tree*
> *Filled with love, filled with longing,*
> *filled with all your life's experience"*

And then she turns it into:

> *"The leaves glide slowly – towards the eternal light*
> *Towards a new road of life*
> *Where a new – a new one is born*
> *A beautiful, strong - new tree of life!"*

Yes, her poetry is like a calendar of life. There are always new turns, unwritten pages to fill! As a poet she often writes in Swedish, but she has also written in german and polish.

So here and now I proudly present to you, dear reader, Joanna Svensson's first book of love poems - written in English.

Svenstorp in April 2019

Per Josefsson

Poetry

The Colours of the Rainbow
Svenstorp February 2019

After the rain
On an island of love
I have seen
the seventh color
Yes, I have seen
a rainbow with seven colors

And I who thought
that there were only six
Yes, I who thought
that there were only six

But really – I have seen
that there is one more

The color I have seen
has no name
has no designation
has no symbol

The color
that everyone can see
As long as they have love
within them
The color
that everyone can see
As long as they feel
that they are part of the universe

The color that creates security
The color that gives meaning to life
gives life its meaning

This day – when I have seen
The seventh color of the rainbow
On my island of love
This day – I felt happy
And at ease with myself
Happy and at ease with my life

The Time Was Not Right

Time was not right
When you shouted for help
everything felt so hopeless and dark
everything felt so meaningless
Everything felt so wrong, so wrong

Heavy clouds darkened the sky
The skyline of my future heaven
It felt like everything and everyone
Was against you

But deep inside you knew
That power and strength
Had not left you
Deep inside you knew
That there is love
And warmth
And security
Even for you
When the time is right

Here Inside- Love Blooms

Outside
Winter rules
Outside
All is cold and dark
Outside
Icy winds are blowing

But here inside is warm and cozy
Here inside – love is blooming
In its utmost floral splendor
Here inside love has regained power

The cold and insensible life
In the lonely togetherness house
Has forever vanished
Vanished from my life
Vanished with the icy winds
Into the darkness
Of winter(time)

I Want to Wake Up

I want to wake up every morning
Swept in comfort's loving arms
I want to feel your nearness
Even though you're not here (with me)
I want to remember all the words
You said to me last night
The words that awakened once more
Feelings
Feelings I thought I had repressed

For my inner mind I see pictures
From when my life was stormy
When stars extinguished in my sky
When darkness swept my lonely soul
And life felt like a heavy burden
Empty, sad and pointless

But then came my guardian angel
And led me to you
Now I may wake up every morning
With you
Whom I've waited for all these years
With love
I thought never existed.

From the Whole Wide World – To Svenstorp

Freedom
With fragrance from all the beautiful flowers of
spring
Is born today
At seven o'clock this morning
Here in our garden
A wonderful, incredible feeling
Has filled my heart
When I saw the happy smile of the sun
And when the lovely greenery
The tiny little brook
Has already whispered – babbled - squealed
About the arrival of freedom in my life

I have felt for a long time
It would happen right here
Here in this little village of Svenstorp
Here I can bloom with my words
And the power of thoughts
On a piece of new cut paper
Here I feel I am relieved of
The straight-jacket of the city
Here, where I feel
That freedom smells delicious
Smells like all the beautiful flowers of spring
Just like a new life begins again

From the world to Svenstorp
To the arms of the safe and secure
countryside
Where meadows bloom
Where the wings of trees
Move my thoughts
To the real world
Where the brook is whispering

House of Angels

In the house of angels
The light shoots forth from heaven
Smells of love
Grows secure all around
Each and every hour
Each and every minute

There you want to be
There you want to live
There you can believe
And feel reliance
Reliance on the inner of you
Reliance on yourself

My Thoughts

My thoughts are with you
You, who found the right keys
Thank you, for finding the right keys
To my heart

They have gently opened
the door to the future
Light slips slowly in
All senses have awakened

My thoughts are with you
It took a long time
Before I could sleep

I felt your presence
Your warmth
Your soft hands

Slowly I moved myself
To the land of dreams
Gently swept
by the soft veil of night

Felt love and warmth
filling my body

The most delightful place in my heart
Is yours!

You Have Touched My Soul

You have touched my soul
with your solicitude
You have touched my soul
with your love
You have let me bloom/flourish with words
When I once again fell into a dark hole
You have lifted me up to the light
So that I could find the right words
to cherish true love

You have opened for me
All the windows of the world
So that I can breath freedom

You have opened for me
All the doors of possibilities
You have touched my soul
with your solicitude
So that I can find
The right way back
To me

<u>Shadows of Night</u>

Shadows of the night
fill my room
Longing lays beside me
in my bed

Miss your nearness
Your warmth
Your breath

I feel physical pain
of longing
in my heart

Recent day's events
have convinced me
That life is worth living
That true love exists
It has started to sprout
For you and for me

It has already burst the bud
and opened up my senses
Imagine that
there is happiness/joy for us

What we have waited for/longed for all these years

It smells of/Its fragrance is love and happiness
Fragrance I thought no longer existed
And this no money can buy!

Wings of Love

Love floats (love soars aloft)
on its wings
Higher and higher
Towards the universe
Like a not yet written book
With the most enchanting words
That become poems
When the most enchanting words
Form themselves
Into huge bouquets
of the most wonderful poems of love

Love floats aloft
on its wings
In great circles
Floats over meadows
Floats over forests (and woods)
Floats over lakes and mountains
Sprinkle thoughts of lovingness
That slowly falls to the ground

They fall
They fall everywhere
They grow with the loveliest words of love
And emulates everything around

Let love float – on its wings
Filled with love – and without impediment

And never try to stop it – from feeling free
Never try to stop it – never cut its wings

In the Silence

In the silence
Like in a monastery
up in the mountains
I can hear my heart beat
I take a look inside me
And I can see all the answers
to all of my questions

The silence and its secrets
Lead to my inner secure me

Here I can find peace in my solitude
Here I can find calm
Here I can find love for myself

The silence – as balm for my soul
Heals my wounded feelings
Feelings I have carried many years
The silence – shows me new possibilities
In the silence – I can see all my inner pictures
And the way I must go

Aroused Feelings

You have aroused my feelings

Like the sun gives life to life

in springtime

After winter's rest

Feelings, love and longing

has broken bud

Like the apple-tree in my garden

I long for your warm smile

I long for your warm and touching

lovely hands

I long for your warm big hugs

You have aroused my feelings

After a long winter's sleep

The feeling I thought no longer

existed inside of me

Winds of spring

Cuddles my hair

Winds of spring

Touches my cheek

The sun warms up my feelings

I hope to see you soon

Because it warms my heart

And calms my longing

I Felt Like a Flower

I felt like a flower
Growing in a dark swamp
Empowered by my heaven
Empowered by my inside

Suddenly I saw
Many helping hands around me
It started to dawn
And your dark heaven
clouded my light one

The security and love
That turned the evil into good
That gave new life to my inside

That was why
I was given time
To see a flower grow after all
In the dark swamp

If you help it
A little bit
With a little bit of light
With a little bit of warmth

Then
Love for life
Will defeat
Even the darkest nothing

Slowly Awakens the New Day

When everything was dark
When my path of dreams
suddenly had ended
When it felt very lonely
and very cold

Then the power
The power of love
Will lift you up
It lies right there
Before your feet
And right before you opens
The door of possibility

Slowly awakens the new day

With dawn begins your bright new life

And all the dark
And all the cold
You have put behind you
And your path of dreams
Will start anew

I Feel Like a Butterfly

I feel like a butterfly
Hovering in the air
Weightless, free – like a summer breeze
Released of all duties

I wear a beautiful gown
Made out of last night's dreams
Feel so extremely happy and light
Time and place don't exist anymore

I sit in a sunny spot
I sit and wait for you
In through the window
Two butterflies come fluttering
They perch lightly on my hand
I picture for the inner me
That it's you and me
You and me – connected
By the strongest ties of love!

My Hideaways

I have shown you
All my hideaways
Hidden in my inner
Deep inside my heart

Wishes, longings, kisses
Have materialized themselves

Flowers of love
smell intensely
My awaited love
has a name
And it's your name
It's you

My feelings smell of jasmine
And you are mine
Only mine
Only mine

I See Your Beautiful Inside

I see your beautiful inside
That no one else can see
It has opened up to me
Only me – only me

I have wandered
the crooked paths of life
And sometimes stumbled and fell
In a big black hole – but deep inside
I always felt there was a way
A way out – of the deepest sorrow

For deep inside I knew
That I would meet you someday
You, with the loveliest inside
That only I, only I can see

For many years I've easily judged misled
Blinded by the darkest clouds of lies
Therefore they could never get a chance
To see your lovely inside
Which was chosen just for me
Now and then the thought occurs
Boasting of thankfulness
That I could see – your lovely inside
And that your heart beats – just for me

Every night I wake up – awaken by my inside
I want to tell you – time and time again
Thank you for being – my darling
Thank you for being - only mine
I love you – only you!

Only Mine

I felt the warm sunbeams
Touching my face
Then suddenly I woke up

I have seen a radiant
beaming road before me
The light was so intense
and pleasant
I felt extremely happy

Poem were floating around in the air
Like tiny mirrors of souls
Filled with lovely words
Words that just wanted to come out

All around it smelled beautifully
Beautifully it smelled of love
Of lavender and jasmine
My heart got filled with longing
Thought of you
Felt that you were mine
Only mine – only mine...

Feelings of Spring
Svenstorp 2019 02 10

Slowly awakens the feelings of Spring
out of the darkness of grey
Out of the long and deep winter's cold
Slowly but surely one day
Drowsy it yawns and stretches out its arms
Gently it reach for the sun
I glance over meadows and deep blushing sky
and feel an enormous strong force
Silently hovering above in the air
then softly falls to the ground

All is touch – all is nursed
by the awakening hands of Spring
All is given life and air to breathe
by the almighty power of Love

All is well and so wonderfully planned
down to the tiniest brick
Colors of Spring – senses of warmth
Feelings of lust
Lust!
Lust to finally start living again
on this beautiful planet called Earth!

Life is a Miracle

In a morning so sunny
I have seen miracles
Don't know if it's dream or reality

Light rosy flowers of cherry
Like pearls and diamonds
After last night's rain

It's moistened by the lust of life
Suddenly – it has opened itself
Right before my eyes

Then I feel
that life is a miracle
Each and everyone
Cherry blossoms, dandelions,
violets and forget-me-nots

This sunny morning
And this lovely season
That all begins in our garden
In Svenstorp!

The Birth of a Poem of Spring

A poem of spring is being born
On a lovely sunny day
I have seen it!
It was slowly floating
Just above cold winters' ground
Swept in a clear morning dew
Surrounded by beautiful colors of spring
The most beautiful colors you ever saw
Sweet scented by lovely fragrance of spring
The most lovely you ever felt
Described in beautiful words of spring
The most beautiful you ever heard

Mother earth has awakened
She stretches out her arms
And reaches for the sun
Gently she captures the poem of spring
And kisses each and every word
Now finally – spring has arrived!

March the 1st 2019

My Thoughts/ My Longing

Mossby beach
You seem so far away now
So far away – but yet so close
I can see you in my inner thoughts
The eternal long and beautiful beach
Long as my eyes can see
Here are stones, sea shells, my dreams and
my longing

Oh, if only I could live a little closer
Could take many-a-long walk
Watch the sunrise
Watch the sunset
Which reflects itself
in the glittering waters
of the Baltic Sea

Feel the power of the wind
That plays around in my hair
Feel tickling grains of sand
Under my feet
And the salty air

Confidence

When the stars are about
to fall asleep
here in my arms
And the fragrance of all
of the flowering plants
Is so fascinatingly enchanting
I feel secure in my heart
Before I fall asleep in your arms

You have given me
All that I have wished for
For so many years
You have given me love
You have given me security
You have given me bright new thoughts
You have lit a candle
Just when everything felt so dark
in my harbor of feelings

The rainbow of words
Shines with all its colors
With colors so surreal
It feels unreal
But it is true
The words
Force themselves
One by one
Forward

When

When I see your face in the clouds
And the setting sun has its most beautiful
smile
As you ever had in your younger days
When you felt like a greek God
When your eyes were blooming
of the most wonderful cornflowers
you've ever seen in the Scanian fields
Between corn and wheat – what do I know?

Your lips are like sundrenched strawberries
Moist from the morning dew
The taste reminds you of your wild youth
Or maybe erotic thoughts
That you have carried deep inside
Thoughts you never were allowed
Thoughts you rock-a-byed to sleep
Thoughts that ripened
Slowly
Like seeds in the field
And became reality
In the end

All the Colors of Love

I woke up
Somewhat slowly
and reluctantly

It felt so secure
And sweet
As I was
In my land of dreams

There I felt
An eternal sense
of love and happiness
Floating all around me

There were small bushes
With small hearts
That just grew and grew
Shining intensely
With all the colors of love

You Have Said/Told Me

You have said/told me
I am your four leaf clover
With golden edges all around
You have said
That it has grown – unexpectedly
Right in front of your eyes
developed the most beautiful flower of love
You have ever seen

And you – who thought
That there were no love left for you
(Yes) You – who thought
That loving feelings had left you
You – who thought
That your life was in others hands
You – who thought
That destiny should rule your life
Like an abandoned ship in an ice cold lake

And then I came along
Like a four leaf clover
The one you had once seen – in your inside

And now you feel – that life's worth living again

And now you feel – you don't have to be
someone's clown anymore
And now you see- that the four leaf clover
with golden edges
The one you see for your inside – that's me!

I Love You, HASSLÖ

Beloved – where are you?
Can you hear my voice
in the dark of the night?
I love you
I need you
My life without you
has no meaning
My life without you
is like heaven without stars
My life without you
is like the sea without water

How many times
must the earth circle around the sun?
So that you
will understand
what love is
How many times
must I call your name
in my loneliness?
So that you
understand
that I love you

The Two Red Roses in the Little Green Bottle

The two red roses
In the little green bottle
Standing close together
Tight tight together

You don't have to say
Anything to understand
That it's the symbol of love
For these two

The symbol of love
For two lovers hearts
Entwined together together
On a summer's day

She showed him
Her most precious hideaways
He made her listen
To his heartbeat

Love's Miracle,

Way Up in the Mountains

High up in the mountains
It felt like heaven is closer
I felt that love was stronger
Between me and you

I saw the golden gate
standing ajar
We peered together
Towards the intense light

It felt like time
Stopped for just a moment
I saw deep in your eyes

That you love me
I felt secure in your loving arms
I felt great gratitude
That you are mine

High up in the mountains
Where heaven feels closer
Where love gets its true colors
Where the miracle of love takes place!

My Nationality

My nationality is human being
I found that out – long time ago
I looked behind all borders
I looked behind all hinders

My heart is pounding
Filled with love
For each and everyone
For each and everyone
I am so thankful
That we all are sisters and brothers
Regardless of religion or color of skin

I am so thankful
That I may see
The human's good nature
Despite the dark clouds
On the horizon of life

I am so thankful
That I may see
See love's shining light
Shining bright

When life is sometimes dark and hopeless

I know that heaven and earth combines us
That we all are children of the Universe

My nationality is human being
Who looks behind all borders
Who looks behind all hinders
My heart pounds
Filled with love
For each and everyone
For each and everyone

I Got the Power from You

You gave me the power
To put everything behind me
You gave me the power
To finally move on
I feel that my thoughts
Hover in the air
It feels once more so easy
To walk
Just as I walked the clouds
When I was dreaming
Hopelessness is gone forever
My new life begins here and now!

(The Light of The) Full Moon

The full moon glows
In the lukewarm night in June
The grass is swept with dew

I sit outside and think
Think I'll go for a walk
I still can not sleep
It feels like I want to be
Somewhere else

Somewhere where there is no misery
Somewhere where there are no
disagreements
Where there is no poverty
Where everybody is happy
Where everybody is well

Is there anyone who knows
If there is such a world
If there is
I want to go there
Without looking back
Without thinking
About the life that was
Before

Ebbamåla farm

Ebbamåla farm
A red wooden house
With white corners
Standing proudly
On a hill
In the middle
Of the Saxemara forest
around where calmness
Is supreme

Fresh air and inspiration
I'm feeling better and better
For each day
Here I can gather my thoughts
Here I can be myself

My love for freedom
Is demand less
And totally free
Here I can do
What I wish
What I want

Meet my near and dear
Gather chestnuts
Pick up stones
Gather mushrooms

And when evening comes around
I sit on my stub
And play with the thought
Of loves' importance
In my life

Full of Repentance

Before you
With my eyes
Facing the ground

Intuitive I feel
That in the air
Peace and calmness
Is vibrating

Nobody judges me
Nobody scorns me
Everything fits
What I've read about you
everything fits
what I've heard or seen
Your good nature is endless
And radiates of sheer love

I am filled with joy
To get to know you
I feel deliberated
For ever
For ever free
from guilt and shame
Judged by someone
For something I hadn't done

White Love and Clear Thoughts

Love so pure
Like pouring water – crystal clear
Has swept away all of my senses
Has swept away all of my thoughts
In a white clear veil

A fairytale like veil with magic embroidery
Made by stars of happiness and morning dew
(2X)
I feel like a pure white rose
Put on the red carpet of love
Afraid to be stepped upon
Afraid to be misunderstood

In my heart love is blooming
With the fragrance of the white rose
The untouched white rose
That smells clear and condition less

So beautiful and so gentle (2X)
That the white love
That gives me comfort
In my thoughts and my life

The beautiful words will bloom
In the most beautiful white color
That smells of love in the poetry land
That smells of security and words of peace

Will You Meet Me

Will you meet me
In the land of eternity
Where love is in full bloom
In the golden meadows
Where no prejudice exists
And nothing is forbidden
Love is allowed
And feelings can reach out

Will you meet me
In the land of eternity
where we may wander
the enchanting paths of love
Hand in hand
Where we may hug and kiss
And hold each other close
Nothing is forbidden
Love is allowed
And the feelings do reach out!

To My Brother in the Stars

In the garden of the night
Somewhere in Universe
My soulmate was born

It was long ago
But I know one day
I will meet you

Often when I gazed way up at the sky
I felt your starlight so strong
My heart was always filled with joy
Joy that you exist

I collected words for lovely poems
Hugh garlands of poetry
I sang and enjoyed just being
And feeling the magic of poetry

So many times I saw your star
Beaming when I was sad or gay
I felt love that growed and growed
Between my soul mate and me

Although we never ever met
In the garden of night – somewhere
My soulmate born in the Universe
I now have met in the poetry land

The Birth of Love

It felt like heaven
Was so close so close
When we met
On the unforgettable night in June

I remember the light of the full moon
Shining so bright so bright
For you and for me
Just for you and me

We stood perfectly still on a tiny hill
Without a single word
I remember the stars
Intensely sending codes
It felt like love
Was born anew

Love I thought
Was not for me
Love I thought
For me had lost
Its flair forever

And then you came into my life

I felt that the spirit of love is with us
I felt the blessings of heaven
I will never never forget
This magical night in June
Where we stood silent on a hill
Embraced by the magic of love

I remember the light of the full moon
Shining so bright so bright
For you and for me
Just for you and me

It felt like heaven
Was so close so close
When we met
On this unforgettable night in June!

To Sylvester

I saw you in my dream
Beaming of pure happiness
Happy and gay
Exactly the same way
As you were
When you were
At most alive

The words got stuck on my lips
When I wanted to call your name
My heart just leaped amok
I wanted to follow you to the light
But it just didn't happen
Unknown forces held me tight
And reeled me back into reality

But I know – that someday
I will meet you – in the heavenly light
That has revealed itself for me
That – I am sure of!

<u>May light always guide your way</u>
To my dear brother Sylvester

May light always guide your way
My dearly beloved brother
I feel your presence

whenever I write a poem
I feel the words fall
Fall into place
I can hear inside of me
What you often told me

Writing is a gift of God
It all comes from above
To write is to capture
Thoughts that are born

To write is to paint
To paint with words what you see
To write is to live
To live in the fantasy of the world

The things you hear
The things you feel
To write is to look into
Look into the deepest inside of your inside
In your life's most secret archive
There's where you always find a poem

Today I feel once more
Your presence, dear brother
I feel a very intense odour

Of the tobacco you always liked

The sweet smell of Red Amfora
That smell I can never forget
We always smoked your pipe
To make peace

May light always guide your way
My dear brother
You are forever in my heart
And please, come visit me often!

I Have Seen an Angel Being Born

I have seen an angel being born
Way up in the clear blue sky
On a downy cloud

Slowly it took form
Its shapes grew sharper and sharper
Pulsating of life and light

The God's sunny hand was there
I saw the halo
I saw the glory
Around the newborn angel

I felt that it was born for me
To follow me
On my new path in life

It felt like a blessing
It felt like love was sweeping me
I felt happiness and thankfulness
For my life
For that I was born

I have seen an angel being born
For me
For my sake
And it will follow me
All of my life
Til my last step

In Heaven There are the Books of Life

The books of life
Way up in the bright blue sky
Written for each and everyone
Here you may read
What you must learn - in life
Here you may read
What's important – to discover
What's important - to appreciate
And not just to run through life
without looking back
It's important to make halt – sometime
To contemplate
It's human – to make mistakes
But important – to allow yourself
And to continue your road of life
Which is written – and predicted
In your own book of life
It's important not to live
As if you were immortal
Because it's written in your book of life
The exact date of - when you will be born
The exact date of – when you're bound to go
So bare in mind

The faster you haste through life
with achievements in mind
The less time you get to live
The less time you get to enjoy
The less time you get to contemplate
To reflect on who you are
To reflect on where you're going

To reflect on what you want out of life
It is written
In your book of life
What you must learn
In this life of yours/ in your life

Whispers of Life
Everyday I hear whispers of life
That life is wonderful to live
That life is lovely to take care of

All of the moments
That differ from each other
Painted – with the most beautiful colors of
life
Painted – by an invisible hand
Made the most enchanted
moving pictures of life
you ever saw

You can not classify them
You can not personalize them
The whispers of life
reminds us every day
To take care of life
To take care of time

All of life's events
Are unique for each and everyone
For each and everyone
Is his own life artist
Each and everyone
Paints his own most beautiful
Painting of life
That creates its own life
As it wants to

So – be alert!
Take care of the whispers of life
Stop! – relax!
Open up your senses
And the most beautiful pictures of your life!

You Have Come to Earth

You have come to earth
For just a tiny little moment
And you shouldn't feel sorry for that
You should take care of time
Bend your knees – breath in
All the fragrances of earth
It is life – that smells
It is life – that pulsates

Without the earth
The flowers couldn't bloom
Without the earth
There shouldn't be no life
You shouldn't be
In such a hurry with things
It's quite enough
To close your eyes
for just a moment
Take a look inside yourself
And admire what is there
And admire what you see

Just because you have come to earth
for just a tiny little moment
You just do not have all the time
All the time in the world

<u>My Altar</u>

My altar is heaven
A late summer's day
I pray with my hands
Reached out to the sky

I confess my love – my belief
In my solitude
Solitude I choose
When I pray
With all my heart

For then it is real – pure
Only the mind, the sun and the meadows
That blooms all around
Like witnesses of love
That speaks out in one single word
GOD!

Everything Has Changed

Everything has changed
Since you appeared
On my path in life

The plants have been given
A totally different color
More clear
More intense
Like the ones
I've never seen before

The flowers have got more
intense fragrance
Charming – euphoric
Floating around in the air

The warmth of the sun
Has become much more delightful
You have brought light into my life!

Last Summer's Day

What a lovely late summer's day
that slowly wakes up in Svenstorp
Swept in a light and delicate morning dew
Woven by last night's moon shine
Woven by last night's dreams
Woven by last night's longing

Oh, what a beautiful picture
I see before me
An eternal ocean
of ripe, golden wheat
That grows in the sun
With all possible golden shades
Framed by sweet full grown late summer

All that I see – is so powerful
All that I see – is so beautiful
My heart is filled with happiness
My heart is filled with love
My heart is filled with thankfulness
To be able to see all this
On a late summer's day – here in Svenstorp

The First Day of September

The first day of September has awaken
So pretty and so peaceful
So lovely and so warm
So beautiful, sunny and sound

He walks slowly
Like gliding over the meadow towards me
Dressed up in the most elegant mantle
You ever saw or could imagine

Taylored by the indian summers' wind
With big, wide pockets
Filled with full grown seeds
Painted in pure Septembers'
Specially selected colors
Penetrated by tasty greenery
and ripe and thriving oat
Studded with coral red glowing buttons
Given by the rowan tree for free
The straw hat
With a wide brim
Made by recently harvested rye
With sunflowers 'round its skull
The late summers' wind rumples his golden
hair
Above his head butterflies flies in lusty
circles

I stood like enchanted
Watching this view
My heart beats fast
It feels so surreal
I see – I dream – I close my eyes
But deep inside I see the same view

When the first day of September has
awakened
So pretty and so peaceful
So lovely and so warm
So beautiful, sunny and sound

Then my heart gets filled
With unspeakable happiness
Then I want to embrace
The most incomparably beautiful time
The time that September always shown me
For always – each and every year

Then I want to embrace my month
And say: Welcome!

You are mine!

Love Will Caress You

Love will caress you
With prolonged eye-lashes of time
Love will bring to life
All reflections inside of you
So open the door to your heart
Say nothing – no words are needed
Throw away all useless requisites
Of poorly played theatre

For your stage of life
Write your own best manuscript
The script of life for you
Furnish your life
With new pictures
Furnish your life
With love anew

Don't be afraid
Of life's new challenges
There are lots of space
And empty pages to fill
In your book of life

So sit yourself down
In your self-made boat
Strong and robust

Built by your own stronger you
Strong and stable
Built by love and faith

Strong and robust
'Cause you know what you're able
Strong and stable
'Cause you know what you want

So set your big, proud and beautiful sail
Made of your own greatest fantasies
Do not ever care
'Bout what others think of you
It's you that counts
And all in life is relative

Indian Summer

What a lovely indian summers' day
That slowly wakes up in Svenstorp
Swept in light and delicate morning dew

Woven by last nights' moonshine
Woven by last night's dreams
Woven by last night's longing

Oh, what a beautiful sight I see before me
An eternal ocean of ripe golden wheat

That glows in the sun - in all possible shades
Framed by sweet full grown indian summer

All that I can see is so powerful
All that I can see is so beautiful
My heart gets filled with happiness
My heart gets filled with love
My heart gets filled with thankfulness

That I may see all this
On this lovely indian summer's day
in Svenstorp!

Autumn

The autumn is getting near
The autumn is closing in
The days are getting slow
Weary and drowsy

In its calm
It feels like time stops

From time to time
Stops – to take a deep breath

When you close your eyes
The eyelids feels heavy
Like the big autumn clouds
Heavy – hanging over harvested fields

I see from my window
Our old cherry tree
Shed its first golden leafs
Painted by
The steady brush
Of autumn!

The Mirrors of Time

The mirrors of time
Have whispered your name
Although I didn't understand
At once

I have wandered through life
stumbled on my days
Days without meaning
Days without importance

Met people without faces
for granted
'With their fists tightly clinging to greed and
desire

It often felt that
Everyone took everything
For granted

Without making halt
And take a look in the mirrors of time
To listen – to the whispers of the wind
The whispers of what's important in life

Someone once told me
That on the last journey
Your frock has no pockets

Nobody has listened
And no one has embraced the old wisdom
that you carry – deep inside of you

And then came that day
When I stopped and turned around
And saw in my mirror of time
My past time
the wind whispered your name
And I saw for the inner of me
Your beautiful face
That beamed with happiness and security
That you thought no longer existed within
you
It felt for me – as if I opened my eyes

You have a very beautiful inside
And deep inside
You carry both our happiness
It feel like you are my guardian angel
And maybe you feel – that I am one for you

Give Me No More Red Roses

Please, give me
no more red roses
Please don't give me
the glow of sun
What I wish for
Is love and security
To fall asleep
In your embrace

You wanted to give me
A peace of heaven
You promised me
A string of pearls
By morning dew
And southern wind
And the pale rainbows'
Lovely light

What I wish for
Is love and security
To fall asleep
In your embrace

Well, time flies
No one can stop it
Time is never
turning back
Let us wander
Tight together
Let us enjoy
Final peace

The Arms of Time

The arms of time
Have twined – with help from the winds
With power from the sun
The new life
That I may endure
In the everlasting future

The arms of time
Capture my thoughts
each and every one – it seems
The arms of time
capture unsaid words
Dreams that I have not yet dreamed
Wishes I have not yet wished

The arms of time
Capture the future
Capture new views
New roads – that I may go
The calm of night
Silently sweeps me
And my strength comes back to me

I feel privileged
To be able to see
The coast of life
And its eternal horizon

To feel that everything
Lies ahead – and not behind
To feel that tomorrow
Hasn't lost the colors of the rainbow

On the contrary

It has become more intense
The spinning wheel of time
Has weaved a ball of yarn
Has weaved by fragile threads of life
A ball of yarn
But only life knows
How fragile it is

I Often Hide in my Poems

I often hide in my poems
In order to survive
from everyday boredom
In order to be myself
In order to be proud
Proud of those who have given me birth
To live – good or bad

I often hide in my poems
When I am sad
When loneliness calls my name
When silence calms my longing
When I can see my lucky star again

I often hide in my poems
To be able to paint
With words – all that I can see
To be able to describe every fragrance
To be able to describe all the flowers
To be able to describe my great gratitude
For all what life has given me

I often hide in my poems
To be able to dream undreamed dreams
To take care of all my feelings
And to give them life in stanzas and verses

I often hide in my poems
Because I feel secure
In my world of words

My Journey Through Life

To love all songs

And old books
Is to love yourself
To love time – that is so wonderful
Pleasant
That didn't pass you by so fast

It feels like you are biking through life
Or going by foot
You will see all colors
And the straight lines of the pictures
Feel both warmth and cold
And enjoy just being
And all the senses are mine
So that I can rule

It felt so wonderful
Thank God I've become
As old as I have
And never fallen off
The forever spinning
And spinning
Carousel of life

Everything must happen so fast
And faster than ever
everything needs to be

So condemned effective and impersonal

Yes, thank you God
I have lived
And lived a life
Where I was allowed to bicycle
Where I was allowed to walk

To pass through my life
In my own pace
And not be put
On some devilish express train
Galloping its way in totally the wrong
direction
Where you from your windows of life
Neither can see – nor hear

Love's Beautiful Inside

Love has no expiration date
No manual
No limited time
No limited space

Love can strike
Just when you least expect it to
Like a clear bolt
Straight out of the blue

Love doesn't mind
the wrinkles in your face
Love doesn't mind
The grey color of your hair

Everything is perfect and beautiful
Everything is beautiful and fine
True love just sees your pure
And beautiful inside
And that's a fact!

Unspoken Words

Unspoken words
With a fragrance
Of my inner thoughts
Inner pictures
That haven't yet got its colors
That haven't yet got any sketching
In the most bashful
Of a first gentle sketch

But it's OK
Because I want to burst
Burst into blossom
I want to bloom
Bloom with my words
Out – out – of the grey soil

Where they shall harvest
golden corn
But then comes the draught
The draught of words
And then nothing verbal
Nothing verbal atall can grow

Finally comes the power
The power from higher ground
And I can see a picture before me
A picture of my fathers' broken coffin

Suddenly I feel
That I must capture time
And seize the day
While it is still here

So I will bloom
In the dark and grey field
The field that everyone
Since long ago
Has abandoned
And grow slow
And cultivate gently
My beautiful words
Til they gain color
Til they gain feelings
Til they gain life
Til they can feel
That life's worth living
On this beautiful earth
Now or never!

You are Not Alone

You are not alone
Even though you can not see me
I watch over you
So I'm always by your side

When you feel
You have no strength left
I hold you under my arms

When you can't find
The right way
I am your guiding light
Deep inside

When you thirst
And long for love
I will send you
An angel

When you feel
Your road of life
Slowly reaches
The final end
I will light you
A candle in the darkness
And lead you on
To final peace!

The Winterview

The winter view has come to life
On Dragon Hill
I see through my window
A new morning picture
Painted with all the colors of winter
Sleepy clouds – moving slowly
Night that welcomes – a new winter's day

The snow falls peacefully
Covering the ground
Snowflakes beaming
With the splendor of pearls

Trees and bushes, brooks and reeds
Are all covered with diamonds
By the experienced hand of frost

Thank you, dear God
For all the things I may see
Thank you for your lovely
Living winter view!

Starlight

When the star's light and glow
Has lost its light and glow – for others
Even more they glow
With enormous power and intensity
For me

Because I – am on my life's last journey
Towards light
Towards the land of love
Towards calmness
Towards sanctuary
Along with love
Where peace is blooming
Only for me
Only on my terms
Only the way I want it
Only with the values
that's grown inside of me

With wings of time
Unconditional love – for myself
Unconditional love – for those who love me
I have finally seen
My true colors of life that matters
Colors that have been constricted
Deep inside of me
Unable to surface

And at the same time proud
Proud to bear their own name
Colors that knew – they were no mediocrity
Colors that have bright and clear shades
If you want it or not

Exactly like love – or hate
exactly like black – or white
But if you mix the white and pure virgin like
With the red and adorable
Then daylight will shine upon
The lovely pink color – with the most sensible
odeur/smell
It is called innocent love

Pure love – like the first night
on a magical meadow
With a virgin – on a midsummers meadow
The colors are mighty – and consumes all
power
To show importance – what you feel
Without saying a word

Farewell

I've said farewell
To the times of darkness
I have decided
I will go only
The straightest pathway
Towards the sun
That leads my way

(Melody exists)

My Favorite Place

I see before me everywhere
Lilies of the valley blooming
As far as my eyes can see
As far as my eyes can see

They beam so intensely
With pearly white shimmering glow
Between the forest and the sea
Between the forest and the sea

They bloom in my fields
In my secretly hidden meadow
In the green land of Blekinge

I feel so intense the enchanting scent
Between the forest and the sea
Between the forest and the sea

It is so wonderful to see
The magnificent scenery
In my secretly hidden meadow
In the green land of Blekinge

Between the forest and the sea
Between the forest and the sea
As far as my eyes can see
As far as my eyes can see
As always
Year after year
In the green land of Blekinge

Angel of Love with Golden Sandals

With butterflies in my stomach
I run barefoot through the meadow
Suddenly I realize
That my feet have
Magical golden sandals

Suddenly I feel
That I have earned
The wings of an angel
Suddenly I feel
That I am an angel

An angel
That I have seen being born
In a valley on Madeira
An angel
With golden sandals on its feet

Oh, what a lovely feeling of life
Life feels easy and meaningful
I feel that love - fills all of my heart
Love for plants
Love for animals
Love for a man
That already lives in my heart
Since long ago

I feel happy and at ease
I run and run through the meadow
With my golden sandals
On my feet

Take Care of Life

No dark night
Is like the other
Although it feels
As if there was

No morning
That slowly transcends
Into a new day
Will ever be
The same as other new days
In your life

No dream
Is like the other
Although it feels
so strong sometimes

No love
is like the other
Despite the stormy feelings
That reminds me of the others
From my times gone by

Live in now time
While you can
And take care of time
'Cause you should know
That every night and every day
Every moment of your life
Is unique

My Mind Often Travels

My mind often travels
To the land of poetry
I often go there
With the intense force of my mind
I often go there
To be able - to be myself
To find the most beautiful essence of words

Words that bloom like flowers
On the meadows of inspiration
Words that reflect
My sensitive and delicate soul

I often travel
To the land of poetry
Where I can find
The loveliest ribbons of love

Ribbons that braids the words
To a wreath of poetry
A wreath that grows and develops
Into the most beautiful poem
Filled with feelings
Filled with words
Words that affects and touches
Words that wake up each sense
Words that reflects my inside

I often travel
To my land of poetry
I often go there
With the intense power of my mind
I often go there
To be able - to be myself
To find the most precious essence of life

There is no Expiration Date

There is no expiration date
for dreams
Everything is possible
If you really want to
transform your dreams
to real life
To choose new paths
See all new possibilities ahead
See your environment
in a new way
Get inspiration
from your inside
Take a deep breath
And strife so
That the dreams
Become your
Reality!

About the Author

Joanna Janina Svensson Josefsson – poet and writer – writes under the pseudonym of Joanna Svensson. Born in Warsaw but since 1975 living in Sweden, apart from a period of 20 years when she lived in Germany.

Ever since a young teenager Joanna has been writing poems and novels. Sometimes they were published in Swedish newspapers, but since then her collection of poetry has grown enormously.

In 1994 she came in contact with Adam Szyper – a polish poet and translator who lived in New York at the time. She sent him her poems and he wanted her to publish them.

During her time in Germany Joanna published her first poetry collection in 2004. It was named "Sehnsucht".

Joanna has written several lyrics which later have been set to music. The most well-known are "Wenn ich viele mich allein, wenn ich viele mich so klein", "Ich viele mich wohl im Land Wursten" and "Gibt mich nicht mehr die rote Rosen".

In Germany Joanna engaged herself much in the cultural life of the region. At an international café for women in Cuxhaven she presented her poems on stage. Even in German newspapers she filled columns in their culture section. Newspapers like Nordsee Zeitung and Cuxhavener Nachrichten.

In 2013 Joanna debuted as an author with her first fiction novel "Tajemnica Medalionu" – published by Novae Res. Her second novel (in a trilogy) was published in 2015 – by Biale Pioro. The second edition of the same title came out in 2018 – published by Novae Res.

These novels are at present being translated into English and Swedish. The first one is about to be published in USA probably in the end of 2019. To be edited by a Swedish publishing company is also Joanna's book of poetry "The two red roses in the little green bottle"

Joanna has participated in several anthologies in Germany, Poland, India, Uganda and USA. Her authorship has also been recognized in different newspapers in Sweden, such as Skånska Dagbladet, Ystad Allehanda, Sydöstran and Blekinge Läns Tidning.

She has presented her books at big international book fairs like Krakow in 2013 and 2018, Warsaw in 2015 and Karlshamn in 2019.

Joanna Svensson is a member of Sveriges Författarförbund in Stockholm
(the swedish author association), Författarcentrum Syd in Malmö (The centre for authors in the south of Sweden) and Zwiazek Pisarzy Polskich na Obczyznie in London (The Polish Author Association in foreign countries)

Joanna Svensson Josefsson
Svenstorp in May 2019

Made in the USA
San Bernardino, CA
12 June 2019